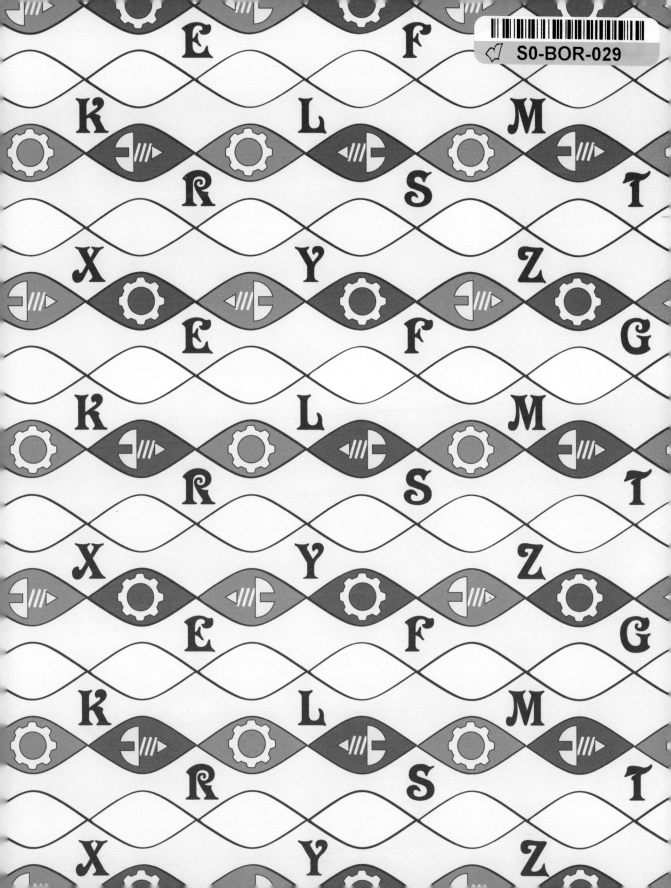

S0-BOR-029

STEAMPUNK ABC

Written and Illustrated by Karen Luk

Paper Dragon Press

Steampunk ABC
An alphabet book of the Victorian era inspired by a retro future aesthetic. Includes a glossary of facts and discoveries of the historical time period.

Written and illustrated by Karen Luk
Difference engine illustration by Brian Kolm and Rae Wood

Steampunk ABC © 2013 by Karen Luk

January 2013. First printing.

ISBN 978-0-9884450-0-0

Library of Congress Cataloging-in-Publication Data available.

Published by Paper Dragon Press, 334 Redwood Drive, Boulder Creek, CA 95006.

All rights reserved. No part of this publication may be reproduced in any form by any means without permission, except for small excerpts for review purposes.

Printed in China by Global PSD.

A is for automaton.

B is for bustle.

C is for clockwork.

D is for difference engine.

E is for engineer.

F is for fencing.

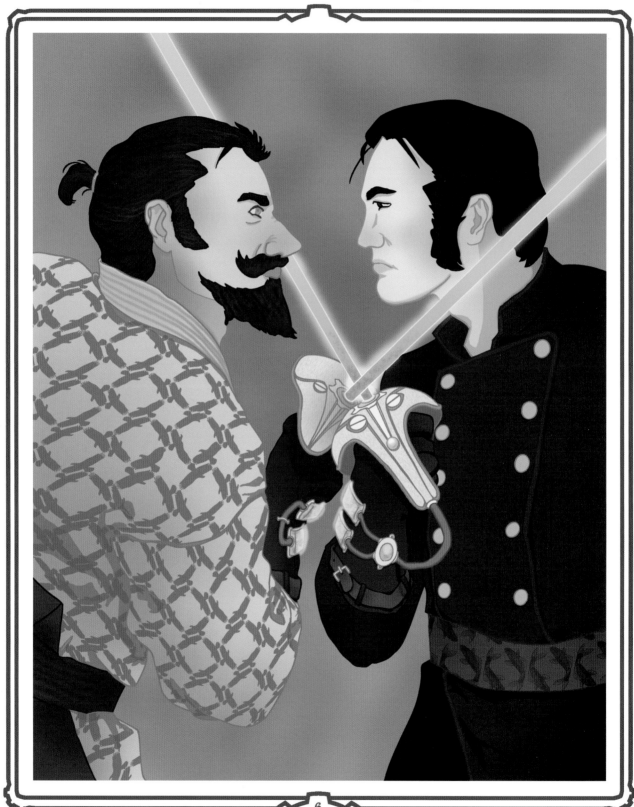

G is for goggles.

H is for hat.

I is for inventor.

J is for jabberwock.

K is for key.

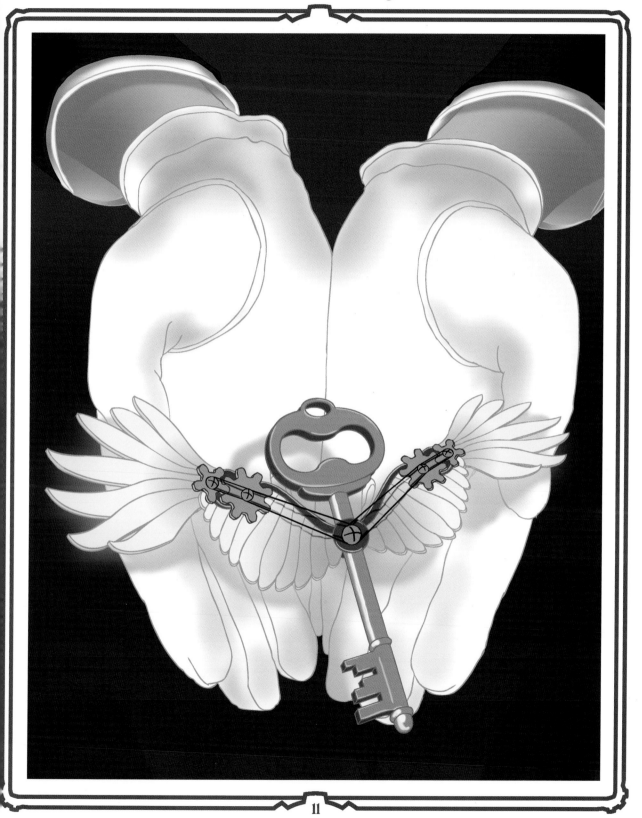

L is for lock.

M is for monocle.

N is for the Nautilus.

O is for octopus.

Q is for Queen Victoria.

R is for railway station.

T is for time machine.

U is for uniform.

V is for velocipede.

W is for wrench.

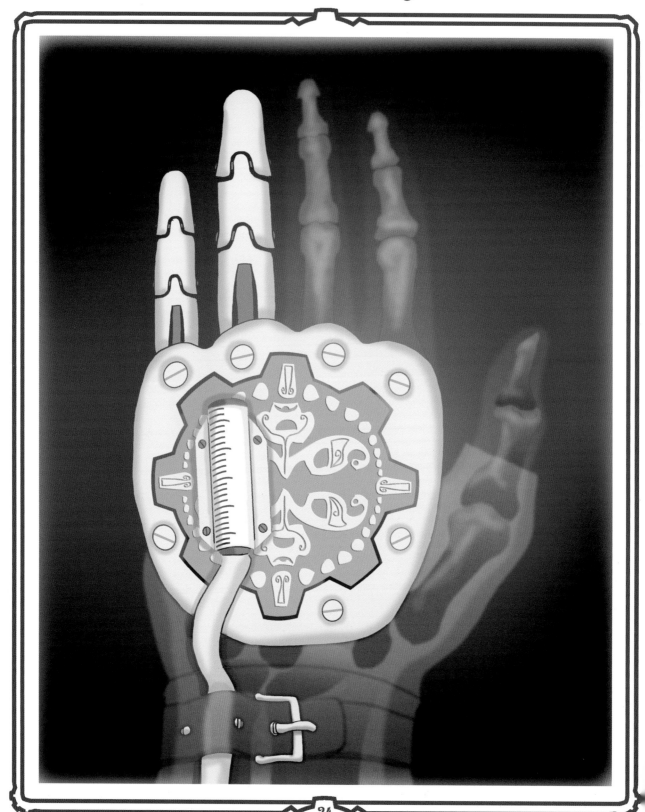

Y is for yuletide.

Z is for zeppelin.

Glossary

Automaton - mechanical figure constructed to work on its own power; a robot.

Bustle - folded cloth supported by wire frame or pillow, arranged behind the small of a woman's back and accentuated the waistline.

Clockwork - use of mechanical energy transfers to generate power; commonly used for watches and clocks.

Difference engine - mechanical, automatic calculator used tabulate polynomials; initially designed by Charles Babbage in 1822, Babbage improved the design in 1845 to 1847 with programming by Ada Lovelace; depicted is Difference Engine No. 2, built in 1991.

Engineer - technical person who designs products.

Fencing - sport of sword fighting.

Goggles - enclosed eye protection strapped around the head.

Hat - head covering with brim of variable width.

Inventor - person who creates devices or concepts.

Jabberwock - name of the monster from the nonsense poem "Jabberwocky" from Lewis Carroll's *Through the Looking Glass, and What Alice Found There*, published in 1871 as the sequel to *Alice's Adventures in Wonderland*.

Key - object used for unlocking.

Lock - device used for securing objects, persons of interest, rooms, etc.

Monocle - magnifying eyepiece worn over one eye.

Nautilus - name of Captain Nemo's underwater ship from *20, 000 Leagues Under the Sea* by Jules Verne, published in 1870; also the name of a marine cephalopod.

Glossary

Octopus - eight legged, tentacled inverbrate that can hide itself by changing color.

Parasol - umbrella used for sun shade.

Queen - Queen Victoria I ruled the British Empire from 1837 to her death in 1901; the Victoiran era was named for her; illustration based on a photograph taken by Alexander Bassano in 1882.

Railway station - train station for passengers, cargo and multiple train engines on different railroad tracks.

Steam ship - nautical ship using steam as a primary power source instead of wind.

Steampunk - science fiction featuring technology powered by steam typically set in the Western industrialized 19th century; termed originally coined by science fiction author K.W. Jeter; retro future aesthetic.

Time machine - single passenger device used to travel in the past and future; *The Time Machine* novella by H.G. Wells was published in 1895.

Uniform - identifying outfit or style of dress worn by members of a given rank, organization or profession.

Velocipede - two-wheeled vehicle usually powered by human effort; a bicycle.

Wrench - hand tool used to tighten nuts.

X-ray - photograph produced with a type of electromagnetic radiation; Wilhelm Röntgen created the first medical x-ray in 1895.

Yuletide - festival of Christmas.

Zeppelin - rigid, lighter than airship; German Count Ferdinand von Zeppelin designed the aircraft named for him and patented it in 1899.

ACKNOWLEDGEMENTS

My many thanks to Petra Brask, Leigh Dragoon, Lisa Jonté, Brian Kolm and Rachel Wood for their artistic input during the completion of the book. I thank Rinley Deeds for his continued support of my art. Without you, my preseverance would have been spent long ago.

My appreciation to all the Kickstarter backers for their support and patience. This book is for all of you!

Karen Luk
January 2013

About the Author

Karen Luk is a drawer of words, writer of images and erstwhile sword fighter. She is a part-time art teacher and a freelance illustrator who creates comics. Her art work has been featured at the Cartoon Art Museum and Google. She is a graduate of the California College of Art with a BFA in Illustration. Currently, she lives among the redwoods of California.

Photo by Jade Falcon

Other Works by the Author

Steampunk ABC Coloring Book
Features 26 black and white pages of similar illustrations from Steampunk ABC to color in. Also includes a word search, a glossary and kid-sized, steampunk goggles to cut out and wear.

Encounters
A comics collection of ten re-imagined folk tales and original short stories, painted in watercolors.

Moon Hunt
Moon Hunt is a comic short included in *Kitties*, a Couscous Collective comics anthology.

For prints of the illustrations from Steampunk ABC, more information about the books and Karen Luk's art work, please visit: www.karenluk.net.